The Edwardian era was filled with the sounds of "the machines with the human voice". It was the flat disc record players that were taking from the cylinder recordings of the phonograph. By 1903 there were over 100,000 record titles available. Amongst this variety wer being captured the voices of many great artists including opera singers like Enrico Caruso, Adelina Patti and Nellie Melba, w was first persuaded to make a record in 1904, recording it in her drawing-room at Great Cumberland Place in London. Discs in 7inch, 10inch and, from 1903, 12 inch sizes. Whilst the cost could be as little as a shilling for a 7inch record, a 12inch recor of a famous opera star lasting ten minutes would be a £1. Double-sided discs were produced from 1904. Continual improvem were made to the gramophone, such as the tone arm in 1903, a pivoted metal tube between the soundbox and the horn. The not having to travel across the record meant that the horn could be made bigger. In 1904 the Morning Glory horn appeared with pe of steel or brass. By 1908 the laminated wooden horn arrived to give a softer tone. The Gramophone Company developed a concealed horn in 1907, and in 1909 the hornless Piann Grand (above centre) came in its own case which justified its claim to be the first portable gram

INTRODUCTION

During the Edwardian era (1901-1910), the nation was in a confident mood. The populace was devoted to the royal family, following its lead in matters of dress and social taste - Edward VII was enthusiastic about the motor car (see cover) which encouraged its progress. Patriotism was in fashion and the higher echelons of society were enjoying unprecedented affluence and a luxurious lifestyle. This was in contrast to the miserable state of many in the lower classes, epitomised by the poster against the Sunday Closing Bill of 1909 (below) which was seen to be class legislation, "one law for the rich, another for the poor".

Behind the stability of national life could be felt a restlessness caused by the movement for women's liberation and their right to vote, which was the main focus of the suffragette movement. More and more women were demanding a university education, more freedom and more responsibility. In many ways British society was changing - women were more involved with the new technology, whether driving a motor car or using the telephone. The vacuum cleaner was one development of the era whose advertisements suggested the replacement of the domestic servant (see left). Also in the home, electricity was replacing gaslight and oil lamps - a great display was put on by the Electrical Supply Company at the Franco-British Exhibition of 1908. Another future could be seen with Marconi's ability to transmit signals across the Atlantic, and also to ocean liners. The new postage stamp booklets were simply a handy innovation.

It was the extensive use of the picture postcard that enabled the British public to laugh at itself, breaking down many social barriers, and encouraging changes like mixed bathing at the seaside, now being allowed for the first time. Crazes like table tennis, diabolo and especially roller skating created new opportunities for romance. All these changes could now be captured on the mass-produced Brownie camera available at 5/-.

British power and influence could be seen everywhere - the ocean liners, the signing of the Entente Cordial with France, the launch of a new class of battleship, the Dreadnoughts, and even the pride in exploration of the South Pole by Shackleton and Scott (although it was an American, Peary, who reached the North Pole in 1909). However, while new inventions like the Gillette safety razor arrived from America, there was growing unease with the increased imports from the Continent.

Edward VII was crowned at Westminster Abbey on 9th August 1902. Amongst thousands of souvenirs — chocolate tins, mugs and postcards — were pocket puzzles (left centre) that required an agile hand to manoeuvre tiny 'jewels' into the royal crown. One innovation was the electric decoration (above), far superior to gas lights, being unaffected by the wind and with no danger from fire. The King's appendicitis had postponed the coronation (see p3).

The Sun's only Rival

STRENGTH

Mazda DRAWN WIRE **LAMPS** combine Strength with Economy.

BRITISH MADE. B.T.H., RUGBY, ENGLAND.

SUNBEAM

SAVES 14 IN THE £ ON YOUR LIGHTING BILL
SOLD BY ALL LEADING ELECTRICIANS & IRONMONGERS

BURNS BRILLIANTLY FOR OVER 1000 HOURS
ASK FOR 'SUNBEAM' AND ACCEPT NO OTHER.

"RASHLEIGH" Electric Lamps

"Sweet Sixteen"

IS SPEEDY AND GIVES ENTIRE SATISFACTION

"TANTALUM" LAMPS

LIGHTER THAN EVER!!

COPYRIGHT REGISTERED.

"TANTALUM LAMPS"

'SHE (MUSICAL) 'WHAT A BRILLIANT PASSAGE'
HE (PRACTICAL) 'YES THEY'RE TANTALUM LAMPS'

BRIMSDOWN WIRUM LAMPS

WIRUM

Strongest - Last Longest

OSRAM LAMPS SAVE THREE QUARTERS OF YOUR ELECTRIC LIGHT BILL

MAY WE DRAW YOUR ATTENTION TO THIS LITTLE ADVERTISEMENT.

THE VACUUM CLEANER

HELP!

APPLY 25 VICTORIA STREET S.W. FOR ESTIMATES IN DETAIL FREE

THE BRITISH VACUUM CLEAN

TELEPHONE 3470 KENSINGTON

PARSON'S GREEN LAN

"OSRAM"

THE ECONOMIC ELECTRIC CO.

"OSRAM"

THE LEADING LIGHT.

CARBON FILAMENT LAMPS.

PEA LAMP. LOOP LAMP. B.B.C. LAMP.

LARGEST LAMP STOCK IN LONDON.

THE BEAUTIFUL HOME, to be clean and healthy, must be kept in beautiful order.

To avoid the great injury done by dust to health, to keep the carpets, drapery, upholstery, and furniture free from the ravages of dust, use the

BRITISH PORTABLE VACUUM CLEANER

which quickly and thoroughly removes every atom of dust without disturbance to the household.

THE B.V.C. PORTABLE MACHINES

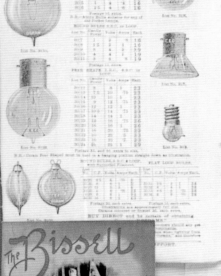

ILLUSTRATED CATALOGUE AND PRICE LIST OF ELECTRICAL APPARATUS

THE **ECONOMIC ELECTRIC CO.**

TWICKENHAM, LONDON, S.W.

THIS LIST CANCELS ALL PREVIOUS PRICES.
ELEVENTH EDITION - ENTERED AT STATIONERS' HALL.

No. 2. MARSHALL'S PRACTICAL MANUALS.

Private House Electric Lighting

PRICE 1/- NET...

FULLY ILLUSTRATED

PERCIVAL MARSHALL & CO. LONDON. E.C.

The Bissell Carpet Sweeper

His reverence the Canon
Has lost that worried look
for a 'CANNON' STOVE
is now installed
His simple fare to cook.

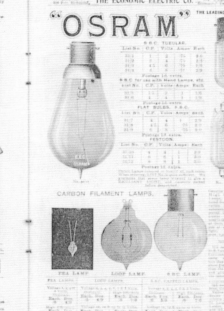

CUT DOWN YOUR ELECTRIC LIGHT BILL 75% BY USING **OSRAM LAMPS**

THE ASPIRATOR

The DOOM of the DUSTER BRUSH & BROOM

CLEANS EVERYTHING BY AIR SUCTION

APPLY THE INTERNATIONAL ASPIRATOR COMPANY Lᵗᵈ 353ᵃ OXFORD Sᵗ LONDON. W.

Vacuum Cleaner FROM 42/-

ARDEN HILL'S **"ACME"** GAS FIRES.

1908-9.

ARDEN HILL & CO. "ACME" GAS STOVE WORKS, BIRMINGHAM.

For those who could afford it, electric lighting in the home was gradua
taking over from candles, gas and lamp oil. The latest household cleaner
the vacuum cleaner. Invented by Hubert Booth, his British Vacuum Clea
company began selling these cumbersome machines in 1902. Even though
could clean the car as well, it was the lighter Baby Daisy that proved mo
manageable (see p3) - would these machines ease the domestic burden?

ANGLO·AMERICAN OIL Co's
"PERFECTION" SMOKELESS
OIL HEATER
PERFECTION
USE
ROYAL
DAYLIGHT
OIL
TO GET
BEST RESULTS.
To be obtained from all Ironmongers and Dealers.

More and more brands arrived on the grocer's shelves during Edward's reign. Amongst them were Marmite (1902), Daddies Sauce (1903), Sumner's Typhoo Tipps Tea (1903), Perrier table water (1903), with Bournville Cocoa – a more spicy version of Cadbury's Cocoa – being launched in 1906. It was at this time that pre-cooked breakfast cereals began to arrive from America like Force toasted wheat flakes in 1902 and Shredded Wheat from 1908. The C (Co-operative Wholesale Society) celebrated the dawn of the 20th Century (1901) with their biscuit

In the household department, Lux had arrived in 1900, the flakes of soap dissolving quickly in hot water. Another product from Lever's was Vim scouring powder which was launched in 1904. There was a revolution happening in boot polishes where solid polishes in tins (such as Cherry Blossom from 1903) were beginning to replace the liquid polish in jars. On the other hand, new liquid metal polishes were taking over from the pastes — Brasso was launched in 1905 by Reckitts to compete with another arrival, Bluebell. The maids get to work with Jacksons varnish stain.

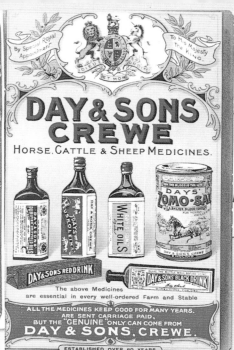

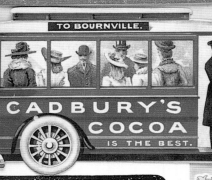

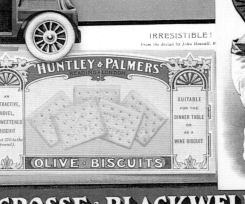

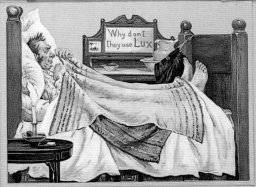

Manufacturers embraced the Edwardian confidence to promote their wares. Motoring featured in many advertisements, thus linking themselves with an up-to-date look, as here with the advert for Poulton & Noel (top). 11

TAYLOR BROS'
Cocoas & Chocolates
THE MAINSTAY OF THE BRITISH CONSTITUTION
CHOCOLAT D'ELITE VARIÉ
FABRIQUE PAR TAYLOR BROTHERS LD LONDON.
TAYLOR BROS CELEBRATED
IMPERIA
COCO
LONDON
HALF-POUN
TAYLOR BROTHERS
MARAVILLA
COCOA
CHOCOLAT
SURFIN
TAYLOR BROTHERS IMPROVED PEARL COCOA LONDON
Taylor Bros SOLUBLE Pure Cocoa

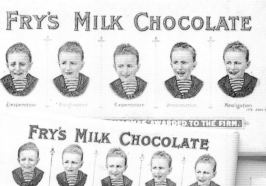

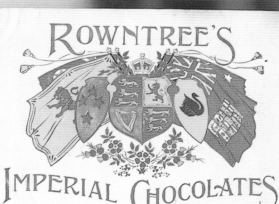

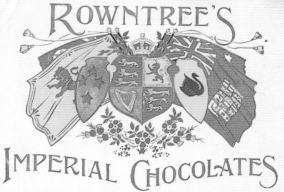

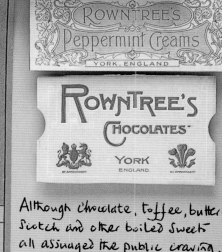

Although chocolate, toffee, butter-scotch and other boiled sweet all assuaged the public craving, it was the arrival of milk chocolate that boosted sales. Invented by Swiss manufacturer Daniel Peter in 1875, Cadbury launched milk chocolate in 1897 and Dairy Milk in 1905. But it was Fry's in 1902 who captured hearts with five boys' expressions. 13

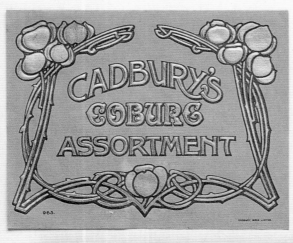

CADBURY'S
COBURG
ASSORTMENT

CHOCOLATE
ALMONDS.

ROWNTREE.
YORK. ENGLAND.

Cadbury's Chocolate WALNUTS

CADBURY

CADBURY'S
Chocolate

Croquantes.

By Royal Authority

The Art Nouveau decorative style came
across from the Continent during the
late 1890s and began to influence graphic
art. With packaging it was mainly
limited to the luxury products, such as
these chocolate boxes from Cadburys
and Rowntrees and the two tins for
Jacobs biscuits. This new style also
reached book jackets (p3). The Huntley
& Palmer poster dates from 1907.

14

Toilet soaps were comparatively expensive to purchase and mostly came in boxes of three individually wrapped tablets. Plantol Soap from Levers, a soap entirely derived from vegetable oils "and guaranteed free from animal fats", was a recent effort to invade the toilet soap market dominated by Pears, Gibbs, Erasmic and Vinolia.

An explosion of perfumes tantalised the taste of the time, floral fragrances with flowery or exotic names – Zenobia's night scented stock, Girard's sweet pea, Yardley's April violets, Grossmith's Hasa-no-hana (the new Japanese perfume). Many perfumes came in decorative snug-fitting boxes, their bottles with glass stoppers held with a cloth top and ribboned neck. Colourful labels reflected the Art Nouveau influence, as did Rimmel's poster.

RIMMEL'S

PERFUMERY

PARIS   LONDON

"WILD WOODBINE" CIGARETTES.

FIVE FOR 1D.

W. D. & H. O. WILLS

BRISTOL & LONDON.

When the American Tobacco Company took over Ogdens in Sept 1901, a combine of 13 firms formed the Imperial Tobacco Company (including Wills and Players) by Dec 1901. The threat of U.S. dominance was thwarted.

The poster opposite for Wild Woodbine cigarettes, now selling 5000 million a year, dates from 1907 and was painted by Alice Martineau. Notice wild woodbine flower.

19

PANK-a-SQUITH

The game may be played by 2 to 6 players. Each
choses a "suffragette" and places same outside squa...
The game proceeds by dicing with one dice and mov...
"suffragette" as many squares forward as dots are c...
"suffragette" reaching:

Square No. 6 — dodges the police and must go back
home on square number 1.

Square No. 7 — the leader takes her friends to Cle...
Inn on square 17.

Square No. 11 — this means delay. "Suffragette" an...
here miss two turns.

Square No. 13 — if two "suffragettes" occupy this
together the inspector feels obstructe...
sends them both back to square No...

Square No. 14 — the "suffragette" here is forced bac...
squares.

Square No. 18 — A Bow Street magistrate reserves t...

NOTICE :— Any player landing on this space must send a penny to the Suffragette Funds.

VOTES FOR WOMEN

OH WHY DID I SING "LOVE ME AND THE WORLD IS MINE"

EVERY PICTURE TELLS A STORY

ALTERED to Tuesday, May 31st, 8.15 p.m.
C.U. Men's League for Women's Suffrage.

VOTES for WOMEN

On THURSDAY, MAY 19, 8.15 p.m.
(Doors Open 7.45.)

MRS. PANKHURST

Will speak in the GUILDHALL, Cambridge.

TICKETS 2/-, 1/-, Orchestra 6d. Gallery Free. LADIES ONLY. Back of Hall, Free.
Obtainable from Messrs. Deighton, Bell & Co., Trinity Street; Heffer's, Petty Cury;
Galloway & Porter, Sidney Street; Baker & Co., 24 Bridge Street; and others.

W. Sexton & Son, Printers, 9 Mill Road, Cambridge.

H.M. SERVICE

VOTES FOR WOMEN

FORM OF VOTING (MAIL USE)

CANDIDATES:
A. Little HAND (Unionist).
S. Mooth BROW (Independent).
D. Ainty CHEEK (Progressive).
R. E. D. LIPS (Liberal).
D. Impled CHIN (Radical).
Pink EAR (Socialist).

PLACE YOUR VOTES THUS — XXXX — OPPOSITE THE CANDIDATES YOU VOTE FOR.

VOTERS MAY NOT VOTE MORE THAN 20 TIMES WITHOUT TAKING BREATH.

The Suffragette not at home

"Well I'm—"

"I protest against Man-made laws."

STANDING UP — FOR WOMEN'S RIGHTS

Hoping you're in for a good time this Xmas

May Xmas never prove a 'sell';
And naught mar your delights,
For when they give you 14 days,
You'll get your Women's Rights.

DOWN WITH THE MEN

VOTES FOR WOMEN

THE MAN: "DON'T YOU WISH YOU WERE A MAN MRS. SPANKHURST?"
THE SUFFRAGETTE: "YES, DON'T YOU WISH YOU WERE?"

Emancipated!

An Oxford Suffragette

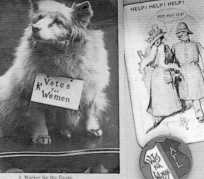

Votes for Women

A Worker for the Cause.

HELP! HELP! HELP!

VOTES FOR

In 1903 Mrs Pankhurst founded the Women's Social and Political Union, although for 40 years there has been a women's suffrage campaign. The aim was to gain the right to vote. By 1905 the movement had become more active, and in Feb 1907 sixty women were arrested outside the House of Commons. In 1908 huge mass meetings were organised and the purple, white and green colours introduced along with games like Pank-a-Squith and Panko. Every situation had its postcard.

20

HOW'D YOU LIKE TO SPOON WITH ME?

VOTES FOR WOMEN

TO MEN ONLY!!

GREAT CLEARANCE SALE OF

LADIES

Some shop soiled, some been on the shelf many years, some spoilt by moths.

AN ASTONISHING BARGAIN.

...

TUMPTY & Co.   No. 13, Always Avenue.

VOTE FOR WOMEN

"TELL ME, WHO PUT YOU IN THE POSITION YOU OCCUPY AT PRESENT? YOU MAY WELL SHUT UP!"

"COME OVER HERE"

VOTES FOR WOMEN

THE SUFFRAGETTE

AUGUST, 1901

VOL. XIV   No. 4

THE DESIGNER

10 CENTS a copy
$1.00 a year postpaid

6ᵈ a copy,
by post 9ᵈ a copy
7/- a year

Published Monthly BY STANDARD FASHION Co.
32 West 14ᵗʰ St.
NEW YORK

STANDARD FASHION Co.
87 & 89 Paul St.
LONDON, E.C.

JULY, 1902

94⁵ LADIES' TOILETTES 98⁵
FOR DESCRIPTIONS SEE PAGES 268 AND 269
THE DESIGNER

January,

FIVE USEFUL PATTERNS GIVEN AWA

Harrison's Dressma

These **5 Patterns** Given Away!

Also **10** Coupon **Patterns** Gratis.

A New Dress for Nothing!
Competition Page.

EIGHT CORONATION POST CARDS and THREE PAPER PATTERNS GIVEN AW

WELDON'S BAZAAR of CHILDREN'S FASHIONS

2ᵈ

EIGHT CORONATION POST CARD IN COLOUR GIVEN AWAY.

Paper Patterns
Skirt Bodice and Bolero GIVEN AWAY.

POST CARD

The Misery of Unequal Marriages.   See Page 14.

ENQUIRE WITHIN
Ladies' Home Journal
FASHIONS
& Homely Reading.

GRATIS PATTERN
One Penny Weekly.

Vol. XXXIII. No. 923.
JUNE 20, 1908.

Contents.

OUR MUTUAL RESOLVE LEAGUE.
Fashions Illustrated.
Boudoir Gossip.
Bargains.
Social Confidences.
Gleanings from Many Sources,
Interesting and Curious.
Short Stories;
Her Absent-Minded Friend;
Straight to Her Fate.
Post Card Competitions.
In the Home.
Our Weekly Free Diagram
Pattern Offer.

A PRETTY BLOUSE STYLE

Departments
N ST., E.C.

No 340 Vol XXIX   FOUR PATTERNS GIVEN AWAY A Smart COAT And SKIRT A Dressing JA

Octʳ **WELDON LADIES' JOURN**

POST CARD

EDWARD VII CORONATION SOUVENIR POST CARDS Presented with Weldon's Bazaar

"The King, the Q are coming."

"Goes the King from hence to-day."—Shakespeare

"Meet at London, London's King."—Shakespeare.

"By these Badges understand the King."—Shakespeare.

St Pauls Cathedral from Ludgate Hill

thousand Ships.

Buckingham Palace.

Coronation Regalia.

DICK

JOHN NOBLE LTD

OF INTEREST TO EVERY LADY

BROOK ST MILLS, MANCHESTER

Coat and Skirt, in Navy, Black or Cream Coating, trimmed Rat-tail Braiding and Oriental Buttons. Circle of Silk Cord and Tassels.
To measure 10½ extra.
7 Guineas

New Corded Suiting Coat and Skirt, in various colors, trimmed self Buttons and Strappings.
To measure 10½ extra.
5 Guineas

Smart Taffetas variety of shade Buttons and Collar.
To measure

ORDERS BY POST receive the same care and attention as goods personally

Fashion flourished with increasingly exotic hats full of flowers and feathers, whilst ladies dresses were filled with yards of lace ruffles and frilly, lingerie type fabrics. Body shape was dictated by the S shape corset which forced the bust forward and the hips back, pinching the waist in. Whilst the wealthy could afford the latest Paris fashions from their outfitters or fashion store, others were able to follow the patterns provided 'gratis' in the fashion magazines at 2d or 3d. Material could be ordered postally from a large number of fabric manufacturers. Alternatively, outfits could be purchased mail order from John Noble and others. In the Coronation number of Weldon's Bazaar (above)

22 eight postcards could be cut from a free sheet in the issue.

The Daily Mirror.

No. 1.   MONDAY, NOVEMBER 2, 1903.   One Penny.

PAQUIN, LTD.
Dressmakers, Milliners and Furriers to the Courts of Europe.

ROBES.
MANTLES.
TAILOR GOWNS.
AUTOMOBILE TOILETTES.
THE NEW "PAQUIN" CORSET.
TROUSSEAUX.
LINGERIE.

REDFERN
— OF —
PARIS & LONDON

REDFERN CREATIONS!
New Models in all kinds of
Dress for Day & Evening Wear

The Daily Mirror.

306th Day of Year.   Monday, Nov. 2, 1903.   59 days to Dec. 31.

TO-DAY'S WEATHER.

Our special forecast for to-day is: Continuing changeable; fair at first, rain everywhere later.

SEA PASSAGES TO-DAY.

English Channel and North Sea moderate; Irish Channel rather rough.

TO-DAY'S REFLECTIONS.

Our ·Venture.

Court   Circular.

His Majesty the King received the Right Hon. Sir Francis Plunkett (his Majesty's Ambassador at Vienna) and Mr. Arthur James Herbert (his Majesty's Chargé d'Affaires at Darmstadt).

His Serene Highness Prince Louis of Battenberg visited his Majesty to-day.

Marlborough House, Sunday, Nov. 1.
The Princess of Wales attended divine service at the Marlborough House Chapel.

LATEST INTELLIGENCE

THE NATION'S SAFETY.
ARMY AND NAVY TO BE OVERHAULED.
GREAT SCHEME OF REFORM.

1903.	Nov.				Dec.	
Sun.	8	15	22	29		6
Mon.	2	9	16	23	30	7
Tues.	3	10	17	24	1	8
Wed.	4	11	18	25	2	9
Thurs.	5	12	19	26	3	10
Fri.	6	13	20	27	4	11
Sat.	7	14	21	28	5	12

PAGE 3

The Lady's Gazette.

No. 1. Vol. I.   WEEK ENDING OCTOBER 5th, 1901.   Price **2d.**

ADVENTURES OF LATIMER FIELD, CURATE.

ONE PENNY   WEEKLY

SUNDAY CIRCLE

THE BEST PAPER FOR THE HOME

No. I. Vol. I.   Edited by HARTLEY ASPDEN.   November 15, 1902.

The Winning Post

EDITED BY

ROBERT S. SIEVIER.

Special Edition EVERY MONDAY EVENING 2/-

EXPERT Daily Wires LATEST POSSIBLE INFORMATION £1 Weekly.

THE LARGEST CIRCULATION OF ANY PENNY WEEKLY SPORTING PAPER IN THE WORLD.

No. 20.   SATURDAY, DECEMBER 31, 1904.   One Penny.

THE

SPORTING TIMES.

OTHERWISE KNOWN AS

THE "PINK 'UN."

WITH WHICH IS INCORPORATED "THE MAN OF THE WORLD."
EDITED BY JOHN CORLETT, Author of "Our Note Book."

"VIGILANT and THE WIZARD."

: SATURDAY, FEBRUARY 18, 1905.   Price

The Clean Slate

A WEEKLY PAPER for SPORTSMEN and PLAYGOERS.

No. 1.   [POSTAGE ONE HALFPENNY.]   LONDON, THURSDAY, APRIL 9, 1903.   [FOR INLAND TRANSMISSION.]   Weekly One Penny

Let us proceed in the Socratic method. We will first assume (in company with those few men who emphasised the rejection of

CHANGE OF NAME.
Desiderating to double the scope and power of same, Proprietors have also re-

---

COMPLETE STORY BY MURRAY GILCHRIST.

£1,000 FREE INSURANCE

The Easy Chair.

A WEEKLY JOURNAL

£5 IN PRIZES THIS WEEK.

No. 2. Vol. I.   Satur

London Opinion

Conducted by
A. Moreton Mandeville

No. I. Vol. I.]   THURSDAY, MARCH 24, 1904.   [One Penny.

THE ROMANCE OF JOURNALISM.   who is not at the core and centre of both politics and journalism is able to

---

SECRET DRINKING DENS BY HALL CAINE

Household Words

Founded by Charles Dickens

Four Picture Post Cards, a Beautiful Picture, GIVEN AWAY with this Journal every wee

IDLE MOM

No. 27. Vol. II.   APRIL 11TH, 1904.

Edited by W. G. FITZ-GERALD.

The WHEEL of FORTUNE.

THE ROMANCE OF LUCK IN REAL LIFE.

No. I.—Vol. I.   SATURDAY, JANUARY 10, 1903.   PRICE ONE PENNY.

THE LUCKIEST TURN IN THE WHEEL OF LIFE

Is the turn that brings luck to the tired housewife,
And helps with the "Trials of the Tub" to cope
By the aid of a Pure and Perfect Soap.

It's Bad Luck

10,000 PRIZES FOR OUR READERS.   See page 16.

FORTUNE:

*"All things must yield to industry and time,
None cease to rise but those who cease to climb."*

October 25th, 1904.   One Penny.

FORTUNE:
MILY PAPER FOR CHEERY FOLKS.

Gleanings for the Glum.

YES OR NO?

ONE PENNY WEEKLY

No. I.—Vol. I.   March 21st, 1904.   28 Pages.

£100

— FOR —

100 ANSWERS.

You simply answer "Yes" or "No."
See Page 12.

FIFTY POUNDS FOR YOU!

An equal chance for every Reader.
Nothing to do for it. No trick, no catch, but a fact.

THE NEW WE

EDITED BY THOMAS LE BR

No. I.   Vol. I.   SATURDAY, OCTOBER 28th

THE VEGETARIA

NEW SERIES. Vol. II.—No. 5.   MAY, 1905.

WITH SPLENDID FOUR-PAGE PIC

THE

CHRISTIAN

WEEKLY

For the Homes of

No. I. Vol. I.   APRIL 28, 1906.

Amongst the continual launch of newspapers and periodicals, the Daily Mirror arrived on 22nd November 1903, the outer sheet of which contained many of the advertisements. Within a couple of years the format changed; the outer advert cover was abandoned and photographic images became the pictorial headlines (see below: Russia's royal prisoners). When the Daily Sketch was launched in 1909, a similar style was used. The railway bookstall was an important point of distribution; this miniaturised children's game included the Daily Express which first came out in 1900. Journals tempted readers with financial inducements, prizes and free insurance on death whilst travelling. In 1908 The Modern Man was the weekly journal of masculine interest.

BER

N'S
E

rated Penny Paper

WEEKLY
ASPDEN.

No. I, Vol. I. THE NEW MAGAZINE. APRIL.

THE CHRISTIAN REALM

PRICE 3D

No. I. THE NEW MAGAZINE. Vol. I.

THE REALM 3D

• APRIL • A POPULAR ILLUSTRATED MAGAZINE

An increasing range of publications gave something for everyone, from the Tatler – fifty pages for sixpence – to the experimental format of 1902/3 with T.A.T. and B.P. "a popular paper for the British Public." A recurring image of Edwardian times was a woman behind the driving wheel of a motor car, such as shown on the Spring fiction number of The London (1906), Pearsons (see page 1) and The Girls Own Paper. The new monthly magazine The World & His Wife in 1904 brought with it a full colour children's supplement, Playbox, a single sheet folded in four and introducing Tiger Tim and his pals. Our Home covered such topics as 'how to keep a man's love' to the cost of hiring a motor for a week: £25-30.

6D NET **GOOD HOUSEKEEPING** 6D NET

MAY FOR ALL HOME LOVERS 1906

Children's Coloured Magazine FREE.

WOMAN'S REALM 1D

OUR FREE PATTERN.
See page 18.

"True Love Comes But Once." See page 563.

Forget-Me-Not

FORGET-ME-NOT

GIVEN AWAY—PATTERN OF SUMMER BLOUSE.

OUR HOME

SUMMER

A FATAL LOVE. Long Complete Novel.

THE COSY CORNER NOVELS

1D

No. 25. A COMPLETE NEW NOVEL EVERY WEDNESDAY.

The **Sunday Journal**

A Story Magazine for the Home.

No. 1. ONE PENNY. March 8, 1909.

NUMBER 1.

THE WORLD & HIS WIFE,
A Monthly Journal for the Home

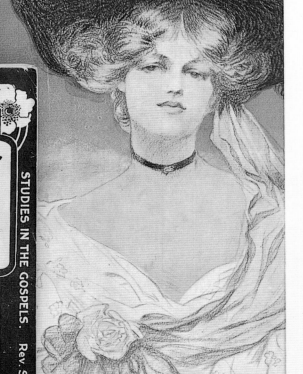

STUDIES IN THE GOSPELS.

Rev. S. KIR

THE WORLD AND HIS WIFE
CHILDREN'S SUPPLEMENT NOVEMBER

THE MONTHLY **PLAYBOX**

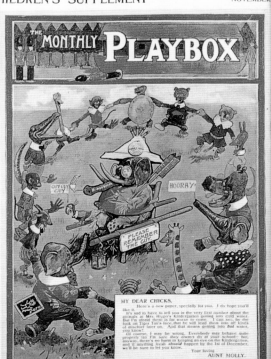

HOORAY!

PLEASE REMEMBER THE CITY

MY DEAR CHICKS.

Your loving
AUNT HOLLY.

ALL THE BEST SERIAL AND COMPLETE STORIES.

HOME CIRCLE

No. 173. May 15th, 1909. THE HOME STORY-PAPER. [ONE PENNY.]

SAL IN SOCIETY

THRILLING SEA STORY STARTS BELOW.

NEXT WEEK THE "BOYS' FRIEND" WILL BE EIGHT PAGES, ON GREEN PAPER.

THE BOYS' FRIEND 1D.

The **Jester** AND **WONDER.** 1d

ONE PENNY

THE KING OF COMIC PAPERS.

No. 53 New Series. ONE PENNY, EVERY SATURDAY. November 15, 1902.

BRITONS TO ARMS! IN GOOD OLD FUNNY CUTS IS GRAND. GET IT TO-DAY.

THE **½ Coloured Comic.** ½

No. 173. Vol. VII.] ONE HALFPENNY. September 7, 1901.

THE **Comic Home Journal** ½ ½

No. 410. PRICE ONE HALFPENNY. March 14, 1903.

DON'T MISS BRITONS TO ARMS. THE GREAT STORY IN GOOD OLD FUNNY CUTS THIS WEEK.

The **World's Comic** 1d ½

EDITED BY JOHN JOLLYBOY.

No. 480. Vol. XIX.] Registered. ONE HALFPENNY WEEKLY. [September 11, 1901.

THE ANTIDELUVIAN ADVENTURES OF AIRY ALF AND BOUNCING BILLY. Illuminated by Yorick.

The **Big Budget.** 1d

Vol. XII. No. 306. WEEK ENDING SATURDAY, APRIL 25, 1903. ONE PENNY

THERE'S STILL LUCK. YOU CAN GET THE PINK OF PERFECTION IN THE COLOURED COMIC FOR 1d ½

FUNNY ½ CUTS

EDITED BY GORDON PHILLIP HOOD.

No. 587. Vol. XXIII.] Registered. ONE HALFPENNY WEEKLY. October 5, 1901.

EVERY THURSDAY. No. 714. NEW SERIES. **Nuggets.** 1d

For December 20, 1903.

Comic Pictures, Serial and Short Stories, Reading of All Kinds.

"THE MYSTERY OF THE POLE," by J. C. Collier, is now Commencing in "LARKS!"

The **Halfpenny Comic** 1d ½

No. 194. Vol. VIII.] WEEK ENDING OCTOBER 5, 1901. [One Halfpenny.

No. I. OF A SPLENDID NEW PAPER.

The Boys' Realm. 1d

Every Saturday

A POPULAR PAPER FOR ALL BRITISH BOYS AND YOUNG MEN.

No. 1. Vol. 1.] EVERY SATURDAY—ONE PENNY. [Saturday, June 14, 1902.

THE BLACK PHANTOM

Our Thrilling New Serial

The **Wonder** 1d ½

No. 126 New Series. ONE HALFPENNY, EVERY SATURDAY. September 21, 1901.

No. 1 OF A GRAND NEW PAPER!

The Boys' Herald 1d

A Healthy Paper for Manly Boys. EVERY FRIDAY

No. 1. Vol. I. EVERY FRIDAY—ONE PENNY. Week Ending August 1st, 1903.

ALWAYS FUNNY—NEVER VULGAR.

THE LARGEST CIRCULATION of any 1d COMIC IN THE WORLD

WONDER ONE PENNY

No. 20 New Series. ONE PENNY, EVERY SATURDAY. March 29, 1902.

No. 1. "FUNNY PIPS" GIVEN AWAY WITH EVERY COPY. No. 1.

THE BOYS' LEADER 1d

...Y CAN TAKE HOME."

...Y, September 12, 1903. Price One Penny.

Part 114. Vol. XVIII. APRIL, 1903.

BUBBLES.

A Coloured Magazine for Boys & Girls

PRICE SIXPENCE

THE NEW POPULAR WEEKLY FOR ALL CLASSES AND ALL AGES.

THE GLEAM

EVERY WEDNESDAY. Vol. I. New Series. No. 58. ONE PENNY. Week ending Saturday, September 6, 1902.

24 PAGES OF DRAMATIC STORIES & COMIC SKETCHES

THE ADVENTURES OF SNAPPEM, THE SNAP-SHOT FIEND.

PART 294 COLOURED PLATE: "HOW HE WON THE VICTORIA CROSS." By CHARLES E. STEWART.

BOY'S OWN PAPER

1903

B.O.P. AUGUST No.

EASTER WEEK
½d COMIC-LIFE. ½d.
The Amusing Picture-Paper for The People.

EASTER MONDAY AT THE ZOO. — BANK HOLIDAY MUSIC

ENTHRALLING DRAMA OF REAL LONDON LIFE!
½d PUCK
EVERY SATURDAY — A Healthy Complete Story-Book.

In this developing era for comics and story papers, the interests of girls were heavily outnumbered by those for boys — Boys' Friend, Boys' Realm, Boys' Herald, Boys' Leader, Boys' World, Boys' Paper, Boys' Life and the Boys' Own Paper which had been around since 1879. Priced at ½d or 1d, comic papers became highly competitive, beginning to offer four-colour print with Puck, 'the greatest novelty of 1904' and then Lot-o'-Fun in 1906. There had been short-lived attempts at colour comics before, but due to the cost they reverted to printing on a coloured paper. Other notable arrivals came in 1908 with The Scout and The Magnet, school tales from Greyfriars with Harry Wharton and Billy Bunter. The Boy Scout movement held its first camp in 1907, the idea of Robert Baden-Powell. In the first issue of The Scout, a page advertised an all expenses paid fortnight at the next Baden-Powell Camp, 'the most fascinating holiday ever offered', for readers who saved the most coupons. For the No.1 issue of Playbox see page 27.

THE GREATEST NOVELTY OF 1904.
1d PUCK
JOKES AND PICTURES for the HOME.
No. 1. Vol. I. — EVERY FRIDAY—ONE PENNY. — JULY 30th, 1904.
THE COMIC ADVENTURES OF OLIVER TWIST AND THE ARTFUL DODGER.

No. 1 of the Great New Coloured Comic Paper.
½ Lot-o'-Fun AND NUGGETS
Vol. I. No. 1. — MARCH 17, 1906. — Price One Halfpenny.
THE FROLICS OF FINDEM AND HIS FRIENDS.

A New Humorous Journal! Every Wednesday.
...utterfly 1½
PRICE ONE HALFPENNY. — September 17, 190...

There Are Twenty Golden Sovereigns For You on Page 5. 1d
SMILES 1d
16 PAGES. — A HUMOUROUS PAPER FOR THE HOUSEHOLD. — 16 PAGES.
No. 1. Vol. I.] — MAY 5, 1906. — [ONE PENNY.

COLOURED PLATE GIVEN AWAY WITH THIS NUMBER. — ONE PENNY
THE ...YS' WORLD
BRIGHTEST AND BEST OF BOYS' PAPERS
MAY 30, 1905. — All Rights Rese...

No. 1 Vol. 1. — APRIL 18, 1908. — PRICE ONE PENNY.
THE SCOUT
FOUNDED BY GEN. BADEN-POWELL

No.1. NEW STORY BOOK!
THE Magnet 1d ½
No. 1. LIBRARY Vol. 1.
COMPLETE SCHOOL TALE — The Making of Harry Wharton — By FRANK RICHARDS

THE NEW ...OYS' PAPER
MONDAY, NOVEMBER 12, 1906. — Price ONE PENNY.

HARVEY WEST, DETECTIVE. — THE W...
...OYS' LIFE THE ...LD FAGS WEEKLY
JULY 13, 1907. — PRICE ONE PEN...

PICTURE FUN
1½d PICTURE FUN
THE BRIGHTEST PAPER ON EARTH
[No. 30. Vol. 1.] — PUBLISHED EVERY TUESDAY. ONE HALFPENNY. — September 7, 190...
HAPPY A...

...TORE HIMSELF FREE AND GLARED AROUND!
PRESENTED FREE WITH "THE WORLD AND HIS WIFE"
THE PLAYBOX
Aunt Molly's Monthly Magazine for Children

...O. 1 NEW LADIES' PAPER No. 1.
GIRLS' READER 1d
The Bright ~ Saturday ~ Story ~ Paper

DECEMBER, 1909. — WITH MANY COLOURED PICTURES
THE CHILD'S COMPANION

GET OFF OUR ROOF!

Youngsters were able to enjoy
many new books. Beatrix Potter's 'Tale of Peter Rabbit',
published by Warne in 1902, was an immediate success and was quickly
followed by 'The Tailor of Gloucester' and other books which featured
Squirrel Nutkin, Mrs Tiggy-Winkle and Jeremy Fisher. The antics of
Buster Brown and his dog Tige, drawn by R.F. Outcault, came over from
America in 1903. Rudyard Kipling's 'Just So Stories' appeared in 1902, here
showing the story of 'The Cat Who Walked by Himself'. Many books reflected
the latest innovations such as 'Little People's book of Airships' and 'The
Golliwogg's Auto-go-cart' with its electrical battery power. Kenneth Grahame's
'The Wind in the Willows' (1908) told of the adventures of Ratty, Mole and Toad.
A book cover (far right) suggested the hope of 'phoning Father Christmas;
hullo (or hello) had become the accepted response on the telephone.
For older children there was Conan Doyle's 'Hound of the Baskervilles' (1902).

30

Children's toys picked up on the new adult playthings — motor cars and flying machines. Amongst these was 'Our Boys' Motor Set' providing the essential accoutrements for driving: flat hat, cuffs and goggles. Plasticine had been invented by William Harbutt in 1897 for his art students, and then in 1900 began to be commercially produced. Teddy bears were the favoured companions for children after 1903; many made by Steiff in Germany who also created a series of character dolls like the policeman and British Army officer with exaggerated features.

Meccano arrived in 1907, having been called 'Mechanics Made Easy' by its creator Frank Hornby since its launch in 1901. For adults, the game of Dressing the Dandy had been adapted from the traditional fun of pinning the tail on a donkey. When, after the King had watched his horse Minoru win the Derby of 1909, a new race game was soon available in the shops, called Minoru. As well as specialist toy shops, department stores like Gamages were well stocked with all types of dolls, trains and games, and also had their own magical department "celebrated and best house in the world".

Just in time to catch the post

I'm in great haste

With much love dear Gladys from your old friend Walter. F. B. Comes.

"STOP YOUR TICKLIN, BOBBY!"

"ALL 'OT!"

A Bright and Happy Christmas to you

I was much surprised

Just a few words to say that I & myself are going strong & in the least downhearted. —HULBERT

HELLO! HELLO!! ARE YOU THERE? Good Luck to you

MABEL LOVE   JOHNSTON & HOFFMANN

Sorry to keep you waiting so long for the key of the organ, but you shall have it before Sunday.

went down to S. Marys at 11 o'c.

THERE WAS A YOUNG RASCAL OF BUDE WHO WAS NOISILY VULGARLY RUDE

HE SUFFERED CORRECTION AND AFTER REFLECTION HAS DECIDED TO BE MORE SUBDUED"

EMPIRE · DAY · MAY 24th
ONE KING! ONE FLAG! ONE FLEET! ONE EMPIRE!

POST-HAST

3RD CLASS (LADIES ONLY)

Fragile & Shy

THE BACHELOR'S TALE OF WOE.

Tunbridge Wells is a lovely place, that you'll all agree,
And when I take a walk around some pretty girls I see,
And being oh! so timid, I think I'd like to woo,
But alas, confounded nervous like, I want to run instead.

A friend of mine's just told me "Men are wanted here in dozens,"
Then by Jingo! I rushed and got on my Sunday clothes,
And then upon the Common I went to take a quiet walk,
And plucked up courage with a lovely girl to talk.

I said "Dear forlorn lonely maiden, will you marry me?"
She started, and towards me turned her face so fair to see,
She said (and then my poor heart twisted up into a kink)
"What! marry a Tunbridge Wells bounder? Young man,
I DON'T THINK!

But I am not discouraged, so I send this card
to you,
WILL YOU BE MINE!
It has taken me a long, long time to write out this proposal,
I hope your heart is still alive and also for disposal.

In fear and trembling,
Yours

Medical Men tell me if I don't get married and soon, there'll be nothing
left of me but a grease-spot.

F.C.H. & CO   COPYRIGHT.   B.

Don't WORK YOURSELF TO DEATH — LET THE do the work.

SMILE at the ups & downs of life the lift boy.

I am very bored.

FOR YOU.

"Bill's not in it when Jack's around."

OUTSIDE THE GAIETY STAGE DOOR.
THE MASHER. "Here she comes!"

One of the Girls

WHY STARVE? WHEN YOU CAN GET A GOOD DINNER FOR 4d.
THE NOTED PUDDING SHOP

CONTEMPLATION. WITH APOLOGIES TO

To soften water, put a little whisky in it.

I am having a very good time here.

"THE LION TAMER."

JOHN BULL'S INTERNATIONAL DUMPING GROUND
FOREIGN SURPLUS MAY BE SHOT HERE FREE OF CHARGE
MADE IN FRANCE

EARLY TO BED, EARLY TO RISE, MAKES A CHILD HAPPY, HEALTHY AND WISE.

"TEDDY BEAR'S BREAKFAST"

THIS SEAT IS NOMINALLY THE PROPERTY OF GREAT BRITAIN BUT IT MAY BE USED BY OTHERS FREE OF CHARGE

Chorus of Foreigners.— "Now then John! make room!!"

LONDON LIFE - The Bus Driver.

TUCK'S GREAT Postcard Competition £6666
A Sixpenny Packet of TUCK'S POSTCARDS may secure you £1.50

SERVANTS' INSUR

SERVANTS INSURANCE ACT

"I burnt my small toe and I work till it is quite better, a burnt toe."

SERVANTS' INSUR

"I cut my little finger, take it very easy, me any more."

Round Pond, Kensington Gardens.

We have just seen Three little Maid. G. P. Huntly Mabel

Over the Garden Wall.

THÉRY, WINNER OF THE GORDON-BENNETT 1904 ON HIS RICHARD-BRASIER.

H.M.G.M. The King, attended by the Hon. John Scott-Montagu, M.P.

OUR PARTY. An unwelcome Guest!

OUR PARTY. His next Partner.

HANDS ACROSS THE SEA

Though seas may roll our lives between, Take this with my goodwill, To say that those who friends have been, Are friends remembered still.

MARGATE in a Teddy Bear

Caught at Newhaven.

My Sweetheart's Portrait

Hold to Light.

Pansies for Thoughts

We are Regular Scorchers at Folkestone.

To Miss Lily Bostock, 110, West Green Rd, Sth. Tottenham. London. From Mabel.

Last Car to Finchley

MARKET REPORTS. ILLUSTRATED. "A Fall in Copper created some excitement."

THE CIGARETTE GIRL The Season's Greetings.

A MILD GAME.

THE LAST MOTOR BUS FROM THE EDINBURGH EXHIBITION.

From 1894 postcards were allowed to have pictorial images printed on them, but they had to appear on the side of the message, leaving the other side for the address and stamp. Then in 1902, the message was permitted to go alongside the address, dividing the back into two. The picture could now entirely fill one side – sales soared as a profusion of images poured out: comic, political, sentimental, greetings, photographic and novelty, some with hair stuck to them, others that were mechanized. 'Write away' cards started the message off (see top left). Many book illustrators adapted to the new medium, such as Louis Wain, the popular artist of animated cats. Postcards were quick to make political points as with the Servants Insurance Act. Some cards were shaped, containing a series of unfolding photo views & required a tag.

35

I must seize the opportunity

WAITING FOR THE MAILS

THE EVER-GREEN.

WE ARE ALL GETTING OFF H

PA BUYS A GRAMAPHONE.

PA PUTS ON THE WRONG RECORD.

PA SELLS THE GRAMAPHONE FOR A WINDMILL.

OUR HOME
THE LADY HELP.
"IT COME APART IN ME 'AND"

I PROMISED MOTHER NEVER TO KISS ANYTHING IN TROUSERS AT NOTTINGHAM

NOTES ON ETIQUETTE

MY WORD, IF I CATCH YOU BENDING

OH! DID H

HINTS TO GIRLS. NEVER WEAR PINS IN YOUR WAIST BELTS.

HINTS TO GIRLS. IT IS NOT GOOD TASTE TO GAZE TOO FONDLY INTO JEWELLERS WINDOWS.

THE POLICE INSPECT'ER

HE: WHAT ARE YOU THINKING OF, DARLING? SHE: "OF YOU, DEAR"

"Buy a lovely sponge, mister, to vash der baby vid? Vot say? Ain't got no baby—vhelp me—I'll lend yer von of mine!"

NOT IN THESE TROUSERS!

Would you like to go halves in this?

Like a nice lerm for this ole pair o'trousers Guv'nor?

"How'd you like to spoon with me?"

"Walking out with Angeline."

"THE AMATEUR PHOTOGRAPHER." TAKING THE BABY

WHEN FATHER HANGS THE PICTURES

WHEN FATHER LAID THE CARPET.

Thousands of comic postcards depicted the humour of Edwardian times. Pre-eminent amongst the comic artists was Donald McGill whose earliest cards dated from 1904. For the cost of a halfpenny stamp, a postcard could be posted in the morning and arrive in the afternoon the same day – a cheap, reliable and convenient form of communication. In 1908 some 860 million postcards were delivered. Every facet of daily life was captured in these amusing situations, whether amorous, domestic or adventurous.

36

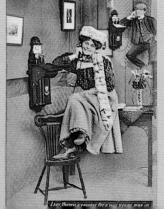

Son and Hair.

WHEN THE GENTLE BREEZES BLOW!

IS MARRIAGE A FAILURE?
Yes, when you've got all the Work to do.

OUR OFFICE BOY ON THE MASH

I AM LEAVING

Are We Downhearted?
ASK "PAW!"

Are ye no' could wae the kilt?
Na – Aw'm nearly kilt wae the cauld!

WHEN FATHER SAYS "TURN" WE ALL TURN.

I AM HAVING MY OWN WEIGH JUST NOW.

Here's to Woman,
The Source of All Bliss! !
Like dew on the gowan lying,
Is the fa' o' her fairy feet!

No end of Waist Material at

LAUGH, AND THE WORLD LAUGHS WITH YOU. SNORE, AND YOU SLEEP ALONE.

WHEN FATHER SNORES.

There's a girl wanted here!

CRUISE

ADVICE TO YOUNG MEN BEFORE MARRIAGE!
GET AN EXTRA STRONG GRAMAPHONE TO LECTURE YOU FOR COMING HOME LATE. IT WILL 'BREAK YOU IN'

LLANARMONMYNYDDMAWR   LLANARMONDYFFRYNCEIRIOG
"A Puzzler"

"He Kissed Me Last Night"

MOONING.
What the poor old Moon has to put up with.

WHO SAID 'ON THE KNEE' WAS DONE AWAY WITH?

Hooked Anything?   (Leap Year)

ARE YOU GOING TO MY PRETTY MAID

BORN ON MONDAY Fair of Face.
Birthday Series.

NOT A WORD TO THE WIFE!

HARRY LAUDER
In courtin' Bonnie Leezie Lindsay, O.
In courtin' Bonnie Leezie Lindsay, O.
And the King he said to me
I'm very pleased to see
Your courtin' Bonnie Leezie Lindsay, O.

Could you be True to Eyes of Blue, if you looked into Eyes of Brown?

Have you ever had a Dream like this?

IF YOU CAN'T COME HOME BEFORE ONE IN THE MORNING, DON'T COME HOME AT ALL.

STAGE DOOR
ON YOUR TRAVELS GEORGIE DID YOU TOUCH FLORENCE? NO_BUT I HAD A DARN GOOD TIME WITH MABEL!

Perhaps We will
pop in unexpectedly
tonight but but I am not sure
we will be able to come over
at any rate we will be home on
Sunday early afternoon
May your Christmas
be full
of uninterrupted
blisters
from E. B.

Dear Ma at Ramsgate.

C.M.Payne

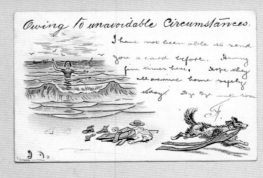

Owing to unavoidable Circumstances.

I have not been able to send
you a card before. Having
from armes here. Hope all
all arrive home safely
                        Bye Bye
J. D.

Greetings from
Gorl...

Seaside Specimens:
The "Saucy" Shrimp.

Copyright : Entered at Stationers' Hall.

PEBBLES

FROM THE BEACH AT
Weston-
super-Mare.

My collection of Weston-super-Mare
Pebbles is becoming serious.
I seem to find prettier ones every day.

Donald McGill

Isn't it disgusting — those men bathing with no flags on!
"Horrid!! Let me look!!"

Auntie dives in
and causes a tidal wave.

Donald McGill

GO ON, DAD, SMACK IT — I WONT TELL...

Donald McGill 1906.
What the fish saw at
"Come on boys, here's a balloon!"

What the fish saw at .... Donald McGill 1906
"Come away Tommy, d'yer want to get cut in 'arf!"

THE RUSH FOR THE
HOMEWARD BOAT.

THE FRESH AIR CURE
at.............

697

Valentine's Series

It's really too bad

Louis Wain.

JANE

Donald McGill 1906.
"'Ere, why dont yer steer?"
"'Ow can I, d'yer think this is a blooming air-ship?"

NOW! LOOK PLEASANT!—AND STEADY
PLEASE.

Lovely

D.F. & B.York

His Master's Voice
"Great Scott! my wife!"

Seaside Scenery

On the Beach, Eastbourne

This is quite
a taking place

I am taking the opportunity
& would like to embrace it.

"Do people get drowned about here very often!"
"No only ONCE mum!"

COURAGE, DEAR FRIEND.

Donadini Jr.

Oh John! Did you see that gun go off?
Er.-yes, Dear!

Marine Palace Pier, Brighton

With Best Wishes

MIXED BATHIN...

I DON'T CARE IF THERE'S A GIRL THERE...

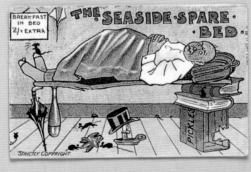

Edwardian visitors to coastal resorts now found the saucy seaside postcard becoming part of a British tradition. With risqué innuendo, postcards began to reflect the changing times as mixed bathing became permitted – first allowed at Bexhill in Sussex from 1901, although there continued to be seaside towns which did not approve. It was not until 1909 that a swimming-pool allowed mixed bathing, at Old Holborn, London. In some ways, the seaside postcard widened the appeal of the bathing beauty. It was little wonder that postcards were being avidly collected and cherished in special albums. Holiday camps were opening: on the Isle of Man in 1900 (men only) and Norfolk coast in 1906 (for all).

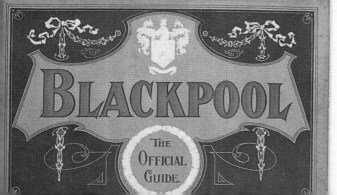

UNDERGROUND

STREET & RAILWAY MAP IN SECTIONS

TOGETHER WITH AN ALPHABETICAL & CLASSIFIED INDEX OF PLACES STREETS & STATIONS

PRICE **2d**

LONDON

REGENTS PARK

BOTANICAL GARDENS

BAKERLOO TUBE

700,000th Thousand.

A.D. 1905. PRICE 3d.

THE A B C GUIDE TO LONDON

AN ENLARGED PICTORIAL PLAN OF CENTRAL LONDON

PRICE THREEPENCE

HOLLOWAY

LONDON UNDERGROUND ELECTRIC RAILWAYS

TO ALL PARTS OF LONDON & SUBURBS

No need to ask a Pliceman!

FAST TRAINS — NO WAITING

ELEPHANT&CASTLE

LONDON UNDERGROUND ELECTRIC RAILWAYS

WILLIAM OWEN DRAPERS & HOUSE FURNISHERS, WESTBOURNE GROVE

CHOCOLAT MENIER

CACAO MENIER'S BREAKFAST COCOA

RIDGWAYS CHOICE TEAS

HB THE SIGN OF QUALITY See back of MAP

VIENNA CAFE & RESTAURANT

KAISERQUELL PILSEN BEER

ALES BARCLAY'S STOUT OF ALL GROCERS PER DOZ. 2/6

TANTALUM LAMPS

UNDERGROUND RAILWAYS

Pears' Soap

RIDGWAYS PURE COFFEES

HB THE SIGN OF QUALITY See back of MAP

FOR ADVERTISING SPACES ON THIS MAP Apply PARTINGTON ADVERTISING Co. Ltd.

LONDON UNDERGROUND RAILWAYS

RAILWAY EXPRESSZÜGE

GOTTHARD-BAHN

EDI DI LUSSO

CORRIDOR EXPRESSTRAINS

WINTER SEASON 1902/03

WINTERDIENST Servizio Jemale

SOMMER 1906

Cöln-Düsseldorfer Rhein-Dampfschiffahrt

Little Guide

to

Geneva

Offered by the Hôtel d'Angleterre

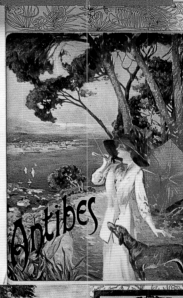

Antibes

MONTREUX

HÔTEL SUISSE

HÔTEL MIRAMARE Sta MARGHERITA

RHEINISCHER HOF NIZZA

THE HOTEL BEAU-RIVAGE LUCERNE Switzerland

THE HOTEL BEAU-RIVAGE LUCERNE (Switzerland)

VILLA IGIEA

PALERME VILLA IGIEA

MENA HOUSE HOTEL CAIRO

HOTEL BRITANNIA CADENABBIA Lac de Como

AGAY CÔTE D'AZUR

Gd HOTEL ROCHES ROUGES entre Cannes et St Raphaël

HALE'S Tours of the World THE NEW STYLE OF HONEYMOON

OFF TO THE CONTINENT BY HALE'S TOURS 6d RETURN

TERMINAL STATION—165, OXFORD STREET, LONDON, W.

THE PARIS-ORLEANS RAILWAY

NICE GRAND HÔTEL DU RHIN

HÔTEL KRONENHOF & BELLAVISTA ENGADINE PONTRESINA

"I NEVER TRAVEL WITHOUT" Fry's PURE CONCENTRATED Cocoa & MILK CHOCOLATE

The quickest and cheapest way to the seaside was by train, whether Blackpool "to inhale the appetising sea-air" or Ilfracombe "the land of sunshine, junket and cream". The Great Western Railway sped passengers to the Cornish Riviera for "Scenery, Sunshine and health". For visitors to London, an Underground map and a street guide were two essentials, while those who could afford a holiday on the Continent found luxury hotels in every city. A cheap alternative was a Hale's Tour (above) for 6d., a visual tour around the sights that included the Italian lakes—"trains" every 10 mins.

41

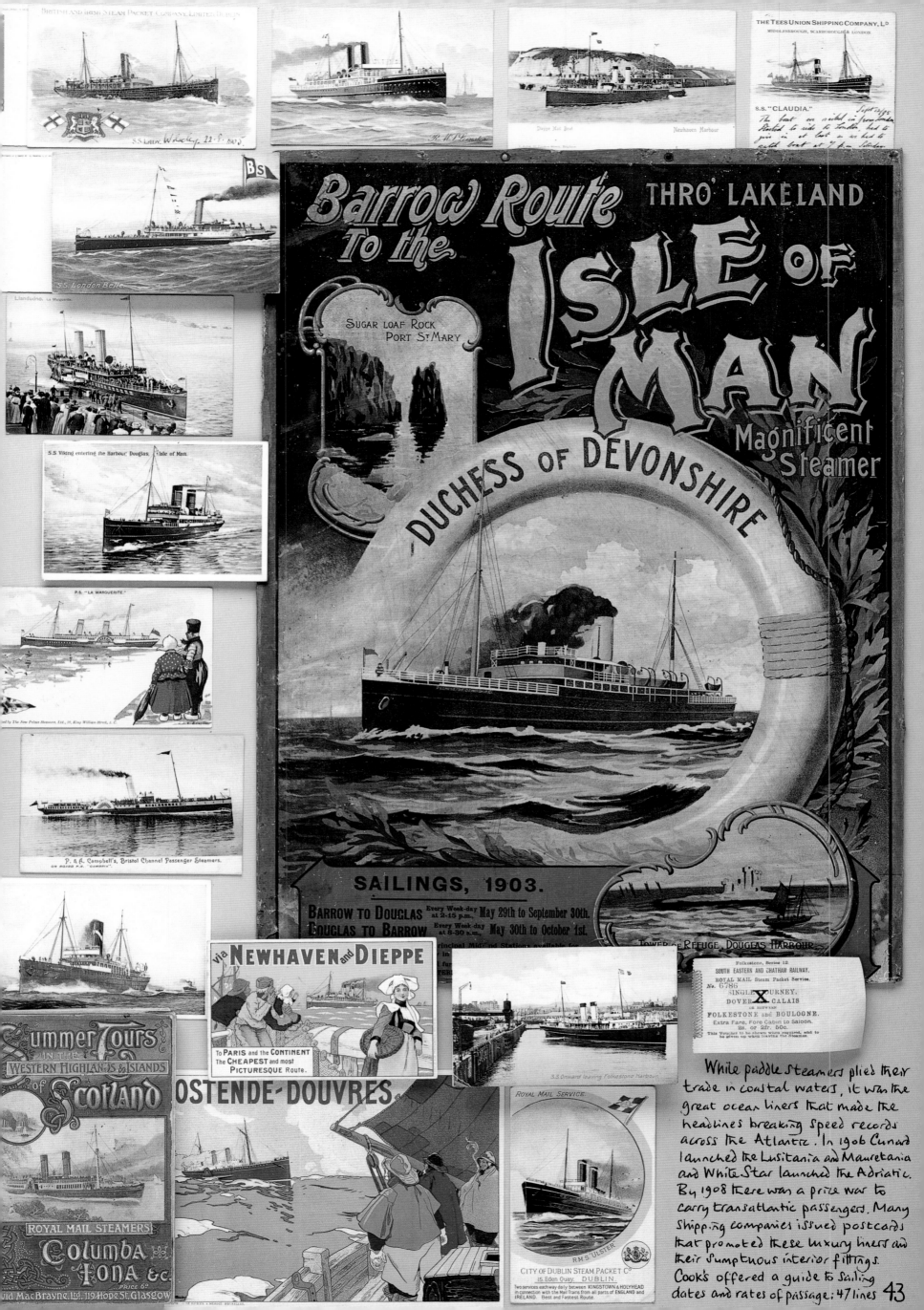

BRITISH AND IRISH STEAM PACKET COMPANY, LIMITED. DUBLIN

S.S. LADY Wodehouse. 22.8.1905.

R.M.S. Leinster

Dieppe Mail Boat

Newhaven Harbour

THE TEES UNION SHIPPING COMPANY, LD
MIDDLESBROUGH, SCARBOROUGH & LONDON.

S.S. "CLAUDIA."

S.S. London Belle

Llandudno. La Marguerite.

S.S. Viking entering the Harbour, Douglas, Isle of Man.

P.S. "LA MARGUERITE."

P. & A. Campbell's, Bristol Channel Passenger Steamers.
ON BOARD P.S. "CAMBRIA."

Barrow Route THRO' LAKELAND
To the
ISLE OF MAN
Magnificent Steamer

SUGAR LOAF ROCK
PORT ST MARY

DUCHESS OF DEVONSHIRE

SAILINGS, 1903.

BARROW TO DOUGLAS Every Week-day May 29th to September 30th.
at 2·15 p.m.
DOUGLAS TO BARROW Every Week-day May 30th to October 1st.
at 8·30 a.m.

TOWER OF REFUGE, DOUGLAS HARBOUR

via **NEWHAVEN and DIEPPE**

To PARIS and the CONTINENT
The CHEAPEST and most
PICTURESQUE Route.

OSTENDE-DOUVRES

Summer Tours
IN THE
WESTERN HIGHLANDS & ISLANDS
OF Scotland

ROYAL MAIL STEAMERS
Columba Iona &c
PRICE 6d
via MacBrayne Ltd. 119 Hope St. Glasgow

S.S. Onward leaving Folkestone Harbour.

ROYAL MAIL SERVICE.

Folkestone, Series 12.
SOUTH EASTERN AND CHATHAM RAILWAY.
ROYAL MAIL Steam Packet Service.
No. 6786
SINGLE JOURNEY
DOVER X CALAIS
OR BY WAY
FOLKESTONE and BOULOGNE.
Extra Fare, Fore Cabin to Saloon.
2s. or 2fr. 50c.
This Voucher to be shewn when required, and to
be given up when leaving the Steamer.

R.M.S. ULSTER
CITY OF DUBLIN STEAM PACKET CO.
15. Eden Quay. DUBLIN
Two services each way daily between KINGSTOWN & HOLYHEAD
in connection with the Mail Trains from all parts of ENGLAND and
IRELAND. Best and Fastest Route.

While paddle steamers plied their
trade in coastal waters, it was the
great ocean liners that made the
headlines breaking speed records
across the Atlantic. In 1906 Cunard
launched the Lusitania and Mauretania
and White Star launched the Adriatic.
By 1908 there was a price war to
carry transatlantic passengers. Many
shipping companies issued postcards
that promoted these luxury liners and
their sumptuous interior fittings.
Cook's offered a guide to sailing
dates and rates of passage: 47 lines to

43

The MOTOR CAR

Polka BY

It's STERNOL DOES IT

Pratt's Motor Spirit always leads.

People like visiting FRISWELL'S; there is always something going on.

THE CAR
A JOURNAL OF TRAVEL
BY LAND, SEA, AND AIR.
ILLUSTRATED.

Vol. XI., No. 133.   Edited by the Hon. JOHN SCOTT MONTAGU, M.P.   December 7, 1904.

NAPIER
HOW IT RUNS.

"You will be glad to hear that the car (16 h.p.) is running splendidly. I have not had a moment's trouble although I have been now nearly 8,000 miles."—J. COSTER EDWARDS, Bryn Howel, Llangollen.

Free trials by arrangement.   Booklet post free.

S. F. EDGE, Ltd., 14, New Burlington Street, London, W.

Landaulettes for any weather.
We can deliver from stock one 8 h.p. and one 12 h.p. Model

De Dion-Bouton,
fitted with Landaulette bodies.

Mr. R. H. FULLER, who owns one such, writes:

Particulars on request.   Trials free.

De Dion-Bouton, Ltd., 10, Gt. Marlborough Street, Regent St., London, W.

J. SMITH CARRIER LONDON

MOTOR CAR GAME

TO BRIGHTON & BACK

COPYRIGHT.   GLOBE SERIES OF GAMES.   MADE IN BAVARIA.

The "ARGYLL"

OUR LEADING LINES FOR 1908
14-16 h.p. (Model de Luxe) £375 & 40 h.p. £650.
STAND No. 36

6TH INTERNATIONAL
Motor Exhibition

ORGANIZED BY THE SOCIETY OF MOTOR MANUFACTURERS AND TRADERS Ltd.

IN CONNECTION WITH THE ROYAL AUTOMOBILE CLUB.

CATALOGUE   PRICE 1/-

OLYMPIA
NOVR 11TH TO NOVR 23RD 1907.

BACON'S NEW-HALF-INCH-MAPS CYCLING AND MOTORING NORTH WALES
SHOWING DANGER HILLS

PRICE 1/NET

ON CLOTH 2/NET

WITH INDEX

ALEX. TAYLOR, "The West End" Gloddaeth Street Post Office, LLANDUDNO.

"L'ENTENTE CORDIALE."

County Council of Middlesex.
MOTOR CAR ACT, 1903.
LICENCE TO DRIVE A MOTOR CAR
RENEWAL OF LICENCE.

County of Berks.
MOTOR CAR ACT, 1903.
No. 2280
Licence
TO DRIVE A MOTOR CAR

"SHELL" Best for Motor

SHELL MOTOR

VENO'S MOTOR RACE
ROUND GREAT BRITAIN.

For instructions how to play the game see other side.

A Good Catch!

THE WOLSELEY

Everything for the would-be motorist — the map, song sheet, race game, auto journal and driving licence — a new requirement enforced from 1st Jan 1904 and renewable annually for 5/-. The Motor Car Act of 1903 also raised the speed limit from 14 mph to 20 mph, while drivers had to be at least 17 years old. Olympia held the main motor car exhibitions where a car could be purchased in 1907 for around £200 to over £1000. The Rolls-Royce Silver Ghost appeared in 1906, the same year that the first Austin car was built. The Automobile Association (AA) was formed in 1905 to warn motorists of police speed traps. The Automobile Club of 1897 became 'Royal' (RAC) in 1907 with EdVII's patronage.

It's really too provoking

So many things came in the way; cold

Urgent

We are moving

In haste for the post.

We were Surprised

I hope you won't blow me up

"MIND MY DINNER GUV"

Our first halt.

I must chance the Gates

Road Hogs!

Look pleasant please

I have arrived at the conclusion.

"Scouting"

I think I will

MOTORING

MOTOR SERIES.

MOTOR SERIES.

TWO ONE-DONKEY-POWER MOTORS.

After a lot of trouble

SPRING, GENTLE SPRING.

MOTOR SERIES

Shall be home late

Awfully sorry — don't you know

Stop for repairs

"NOW I MUST HAVE YOUR NAME AND ADDRESS, SO ITS NO USE TRYING TO HIDE YOURSELF!"

THE SUBLIM

BANG

THE PLEASURES OF MOTORING

DEAF OLD GENT: THERE, THAT'S THE FIRST TIME I'VE HEARD THE NIGHTINGALE THIS YEAR!

Postcards reflected the trials and tribulations of motoring, especially the breakdowns and accidents. There was also much humour made from the woes of pedestrians when involved in road mishaps, and the problems encountered by policemen controlling the increasing road traffic. By lucky chance, the picture postcard was on hand to record the early days of motoring history. Wealthy car owners could afford chauffeurs who would fix any breakdown. By 1904 there were 8,500 private cars on the road, doubling in a year. In 1909 a petrol tax added 3d a gallon.

46

In this series of postcards drawn by Chas Crombie, the numerous regulations of the 1903 Motor Car Act were ridiculed with pictorial humour. The registration of vehicles became compulsory, with 28,000 in 1904 - the number plate A1 was allocated to Earl Russell. Registration cost £1.

AEROPLANE RACE

ROUND THE BRITISH EMPIRE.

BRITISH MANUFACTURE.

THE ILLUSTRATED
LONDON NEWS

REGISTERED AT THE GENERAL POST OFFICE AS A NEWSPAPER.

No. 3672.—VOL. CXXXV. SATURDAY, SEPTEMBER 4, 1909. With Special Coloured Supplement—Mont Blanc. SIXPENCE

THE LONGEST FLIGHT EVER MADE ON A HEAVIER-THAN-AIR MACHINE: MR. HENRY FARMAN FLYING 118 MILES IN 3½ HOURS AT RHEIMS.

69. Blériot about to land at Dover after crossing the Channel in his aeroplane.—L.L.

Blériot Crossing the Channel 25th July 1909.

Blériot Monoplane.

A BLÉRIOT MONOPLANE.

BLERIOT'S CROSS-CHANNEL FLIGHT

AERONAUTICS
Edited by MAJOR B. BADEN-POWELL, F.R.A.S., F.R.Met.Soc., and J. H. LEDEBOER, B.A.

Vol. II. No. 8 AUGUST, 1909. Entered at Stationers' Hall THREEPENCE NET

Contents

THE FIRST CROSS-CHANNEL FLIGHT (Fully Illustrated)
THE MONOPLANE "BLERIOT XI." (Illustrated)
HUBERT LATHAM'S ATTEMPTS TO CROSS THE CHANNEL (Illustrated)
Events

THE CHANNEL FLIGHT: SOME PERSONAL IMPRESSIONS. By Harry Delacombe
"AERONAUTICS" DESIGN COMPETITION: The Winning Designs

BLACK & WHITE
VOL. XXXVIII SATURDAY, AUGUST 28, 1909. PRICE SIXPENCE

Another World's Record.

The AERO
1D

No. 26. Vol. I. Tuesday, Nov. 16th, 1909.

AVIATION WEEK AT RHEIMS.

Pauline Chase.

Doncaster Aviation Meeting.

Under the Rules of the International Aeronautical Federation

DONCASTER CUP—For the best total in the Trials.

MONEY PRIZES & CUPS such as Great Northern Railway Cup, Doncaster Tradesmen's Cup, Chairman's Cup, Goldsmiths & Silversmiths, Ltd. Cup, Women's Aerial League Gold Medal, B.D.V. Cup, and others will be given for Distance, longest time in Air, Speed, Height, Passenger Carrying, best Cross-Country Journey, best Flight by British Aviator with British Built Machine.

The sum of £12,000 has been paid to Aviators competing at the Doncaster Meeting, and in addition valuable Cups are offered to C

THE FIRST FLYING MEETING IN ENGLAND
DONCASTER AVIATION CONTEST
THE OFFICIAL PROGRAMME

OCTOBER 1909
Friday 15
Saturday 16

OF EVENTS AT THE DONCASTER AERODROME

CONTENTS:
COMMITTEE. SIGNALS.
ARRANGEMENTS. RULES OF D.A.C.

Price 3d.

Best on Earth
Best in the Air

Motor
SPIRIT

THE FIRST AVIATION WEEK HELD IN GT BRITAIN

BLACKPOOL OCT 18-24 1909

SOUVENIR OF BLACKPOOL AVIATION WEEK 1909.

While the airship captured the imagination of the future, it was the aeroplane that became the aviator's dream. The Wright brothers from the USA made the first powered and controlled flights in 1903, and in 1908 Wilbur Wright demonstrated his 'plane in France. Within a year, Louis Blériot had flown across the English Channel to claim the £1000 prize offered by the Daily Mail.

Two great crazes of the Edwardian era were those of table tennis and diabolo. Table tennis had been played during the 1890s, but it was between 1901 and 1904 (now also being called ping-pong) that the craze swept Britain - and America from 1902. The cricketer W.G. Grace was a great enthusiast, especially when rain stopped play outside. Specially printed postcards invited friends round to play. Soon after the ping-pong craze had subsided, diabolo-mania replaced it, and during 1907 and 1908 every street, park, office and home was unsafe.

"RINKING" — "WHEN AWKWARDNESS IS USEFUL!"

"NOT HURT I HOPE!!" "NOT MUCH" SAID SHE, "BUT TAKE YOUR WEIGHT FROM OFF MY KNEE!"

RINKING — RETIRING FROM THE BAR.

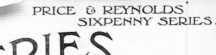

OLYMPIA KENSINGTON W. — OPENS DEC 4 — OPENS DEC 4
3 Sessions Daily. The Samuel Winslow Ball Bearing Steel Skates used exclusively.
Military Band. Afternoon Teas.
Managing Directors: C. P. CRAWFORD F. A. WILKINS.

"RINKING" — "I BECAME GREATLY ATTACHED TO A YOUNG LADY I MET AT THE RINK!"

LEADING HIM ON.

PRICE & REYNOLDS' SIXPENNY SERIES.

THE RINKERIES Lancers

ARRANGED BY TOM GAGGS

Introducing the following Popular Melodies

Dance of the Teddy Bears · Chorus next Verse · You don't know what you can do till you try · Mother is the Leader of Society · I wouldn't mind waltzing the Waltz Dream · Fiz with you · You don't know you're alive until you're forty-five · All I want is Traffic Square · What does it matter what the house is like · Rose and the Iris · The Old ... the best of all · Share my Pagoda with me · Dear Loch Lomond · Maisie ... her Teddy Bear · She was a Grand Old Lady · Reggie · Do, Re, Mi, ...

Copyright.
A. E. WOODWARD, 77 High St. Cheltenham.

LONDON:
PRICE & REYNOLDS,
41, BERNERS STREET, W.

PRICE 6ᴰ
NO DISCOUNT ALLOWED

"RINKING" — "WHEN BERTIE THINKS SKATING IS NOT A PLEASURE!"

NEVER LOSE AN OPPORTUNITY.

"RINKING" — "OH GEORGE THIS IS SO SUDDEN!!"

DON'T GO DRINKING WHEN YOU'RE RINKING.

"RINKING" — "SORRY IF I INTRUDE!"

FROLICS AT THE RINK.
PA AND FAMILY ON SKATES, PA DEVELOPS A SPEED OF 30 MILES AN HOUR AND FINISHES UP THROUGH A BRICK WALL.
SYLKUSS

"RINKING" — "MY STYLE IS CAUSING A SENSATION!"

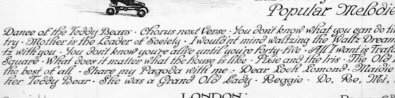

I WISH SHE'D DO THIS WITH...

RINK RULES Nº 6
In putting on skates see that the buckles are upon the outside of the foot.

ON BENDED KNEE, BEFORE WE PART, COME AND TELL ME NOW YOU DO, YOU DO NOT KNOW HOW SWEET IT FEELS A LIFE OF LOVE AND JOY ON WHEELS

When Mary went upon the Rink And came a fearful cropper, The Boys, who rushed to see the fun, Said, "Harem Skirts ain't proper."

AND HE TOLD HER HE'D SPRAINED...

The pursuit of roller skating, or 'rinking' as it became widely known, had begun in the 1880s, but the craze had lapsed. In 1904 a revival began, encouraged by advances in the ball-bearing skate which greatly enhanced the smoothness and thus the pleasure of roller skating. Special rinks were quickly erected around the country which became havens for courting couples. Many rinks had bar facilities - there was a saying "don't go drinking when you're rinking". There was also a soft drink called Rinko (see p 8). The skate itself would be attached to a stout boot by means of a clamp at the front and a strap at the back (see opposite corner). For those who saw roller skating as a sport, rather than a pastime, championships were held at Olympia for speed, fancy, trick and figure skating, even roller polo. As ever, picture postcard humour found fun at every opportunity.

BE CAREFUL WHEN ON THE RINK. NOT TO LOSE YOUR HEAD
LUCKY I FELL ON SOMETHING SOFT

ROLLER SKATING — LOOK WHERE YOU'RE GOING.

Now for the Bump!

MA FELL A FLOP ON THE POOR OLD 'COP' WHO SHOUTED.— MIND MY STAFF!!

"Remember you skate on your ... not on your head."

52

BEGINNING

RINKING

My Word! IF I CATCH YOU BENDING

Schürer's famed Two-Step, "Mamie, I love yer," post free 1/-

AREN'T I DISPLAYING MY AGILITY? WELL-ER-NOT QUITE -BUT VERY NEARLY!!

I TRIED TO HOLD MY OWN AT THE RINK.

THE HIGHLAND FLING!

WHAT HO! SHE BUMPS!

RINKING
A WEEKLY RINKS JOURNAL
Devoted to the Interests of the Roller Skating World.

Vol. I. No. 16. THURSDAY, JANUARY 20, 1910. ONE PENNY.

RINK ORCHESTRAS

KEITH, PROWSE & Co LTD
AUTOMATIC DEPT. 38 BERNERS ST. LONDON. W.

Belle o' the Rink
Waltz
Leopold D. Schürer

By the same composer
Woodland Voices, 1/6
Veneria Tarantelle, 1/6
Poppies, 1/6
Alma March, 1/6
Gordon Highlanders, 1/6
Phyllis Waltz, 1/6
Happy Haymakers, 1/6
Cornflowers, 1/6
Old Mill,
Queen of
Lady Marj
Meadow
Merry Mi

COPYRIGHT
PRICE 3/-

GLASGOW.
MOZART ALLAN,
60 SOUTH PORTLAND STREET.

"RINKING"
"CAUSE AND EFFECT!"

"RINKING"
THE LOOKER-ON SEES MOST OF THE GAME!!

"RINKING"
...DO YOU REVERSE?

...DON'T FLING YOUR ARMS ABOUT, ... HAVE CONFIDENCE

ALL SKATERS PLEASE REVERSE OBSERVE THESE SIGNALS

WE MET AT THE RINK.

RINKING
"OO'S DOT DE SKATES IN DE WRONG PLACE!"

ROLLER SKATING
HE SLIPPED ON A HAIRPIN.

SPALDING'S ATHLETIC LIBRARY
Price 6d Nett.
ROLLER SKATING GUIDE
BRITISH SPORTS PUBLISHING COMPANY Ltd
2 & 3, Hind Court, Fleet Street, London. E.C.

Group XIII. No 33

Hesitation.

"RINKING"
NEVER AGAIN!"

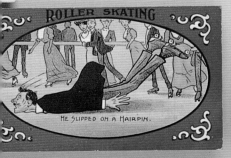

terrible time at the Rink."

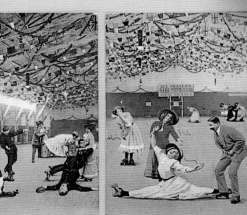

AN AWKWARD SLIP.

I DO LIKE TO BE WHERE THE GIRLS ARE.

I HAD MY GIRL DOWN AT THE RINK.

I'VE DISCOVERED THE POLE, AND MET COOK THERE.

We all skate at Brighton
From

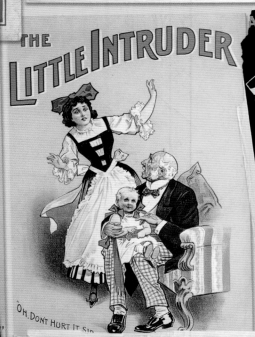

ALI BABA AND THE FORTY THIEVES.

Grand CINEMATOGRAPH PANTOMIME

New Theatre,
WHITEWASHING
JULIA
MONDAY, OCT. 19
FOR THREE NIGHTS
BY HENRY ARTHUR JONES

NEW THEATRE
CAMBRIDGE
MONDAY, NOV. 2nd, 1903. FOR THREE NIGHTS ONLY.
MR TOM B. DAVIS'S COMPANY.
THE MEDAL AND THE MAID
Book by OWEN HALL.
Lyrics by CHAS H. TAYLOR.
Additional Lyrics by GEO. ROLLITT & PAUL RUBENS. Music by SIDNEY JONES.
PRODUCED BY SIDNEY ELLISON.

CHARLEY'S AUNT

"FLYING NOW BUT STILL RUNNING"

NEW THEATRE, Cambridge
"SUNDAY"
THE SUCCESS OF THE LONDON SEASON AT THE COMEDY THEATRE
FRED TERRY AND MISS JULIA NEILSON

NEW THEATRE, CAMBRIDGE
THURSDAY, MAY 12.   THREE NIGHTS AND SATURDAY MATINEE.

JOSEPH ENTANGLED
BY HENRY ARTHUR JONES.
FROM THE HAYMARKET THEATRE, LONDON

DRURY LANE PANTOMIME
THE WHITE CAT
WRITTEN & INVENTED BY HICKORY WOOD & ARTHUR

THE FASCINATING MR VANDERVELDT
NEW THEATRE, CAMBRIDGE
THURSDAY, NOVEMBER 15, THREE NIGHTS, AND SATURDAY MATINEE.

NEW THEATRE, Cambridge. | Monday, Oct. 24, and Two Following Nights

SATURDAY TO MONDAY
FROM THE ST JAMES'S THEATRE · LONDON BY ARRANGEMENT WITH MR GEORGE ALEXANDER
By Frederick Fenn and Richard Pryce
—kison's Company

COLLIN'S
STALLS
ISLINGTON GREEN, N.

PETER PAN
KEEPSAKE

THE THEATRE
A MAGAZINE FOR PLAYGOERS
No 1. Vol. I.
6D NET MONTHLY
Miss Marie Tempest in .... "Penelope."

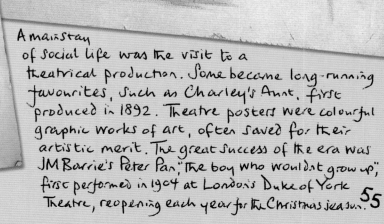

A mainstay
of social life was the visit to a
theatrical production. Some became long-running
favourites, such as Charley's Aunt, first
produced in 1892. Theatre posters were colourful
graphic works of art, often saved for their
artistic merit. The great success of the era was
JM Barrie's Peter Pan "The boy who wouldn't grow up",
first performed in 1904 at London's Duke of York
Theatre, reopening each year for the Christmas season.

55

MILITARY EXHIBITION
EARL'S COURT
1901 PROGRAMME
PRICE 2d
IMRE KIRALFY — DIRECTOR GENERAL

PARIS IN LONDON
EARLS COURT 1902
IMRE KIRALFY DIRECTOR GENERAL
2d
DAILY PROGRAMME
GALE & POLDEN, LTD., LITHO., 2, AMEN CORNER, LONDON, E.C.

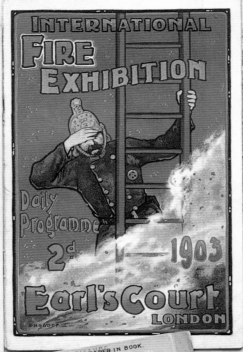

1906 · TO-DAY'S EVENTS ON COLOURED PAPER IN BOOK

INTERNATIONAL FIRE EXHIBITION
Daily Programme 2d — 1903
Earl's Court LONDON

IMPERIAL-ROYAL
AUSTRIAN EXHIBITION 1906
DAILY PROGRAMME
2d
EARL'S COURT

HUNGARIAN

FAR

WIGGLE-WOGGLE TWO-STEP
BY
W.S. GEORGE

ROYAL Naval & Military TOURNAMENT
OLYMPIA
FROM MAY 17TH TO JUNE 2ND
6d
Under the Patronage of His Most Gracious Majesty the King and with the sanction of The Lords Commissioners of His Majesty's Admiralty and the Army Council
PRICE

Crystal Palace
PROGRAMME
2d
GUY WHITTEN & CO. CRYSTAL PALACE AND AT BATTERSEA

FROM THE
BLACKPOOL
WINTER GARDENS
GENERAL MANAGER, MR. JNO R. HUDDLESTONE
'XMAS SEASON, 1902-3
Copyright by War...
Clarkson's Scrinzi's Tr...
ZOO HIPPODROME, GLASGOW.
GRAND Spectacular BALLET
FROM MONTE CARLO TO JAPAN

MADAME TUSSAUD'S EXHIBITION
GUIDE
WRITTEN BY GEO. AUGUSTUS SALA
MADAME TUSSAUD & SONS, LTD
BAKER ST. STATION, LONDON, W.
PRICE SIXPENCE.

Belle Vue GARDENS.
OFFICIAL GUIDE 1d

OFFICIAL GUIDE
Belle Vue Gardens
MANCHESTER
1d

SOUVENIR OF THE
MARATHON RACE
FROM WINDSOR CASTLE TO THE STADIUM.
SHEPHERDS BUSH.
FRIDAY, JULY 24, 1908.

Fifty-seven picked Runners, representing Seventeen different nations, will start from Windsor Great Park at HALF-PAST TWO. The first man to enter the Stadium, after running once round the track will be acclaimed the victor in the greatest long-distance event in the history of the world.

The following time-table gives the approximate times at which the runners will pass different places on the course:—

	P.M.
Start —	2.30
Slough	2.47
Uxbridge	3.20
Ruislip	3.50
Harrow	4.10
Wembley	4.30
Harlesden	4.45
Wormwood Scrubbs	4.54
The Stadium	5.5

A rocket or gun will be fired on reaching Willesden Junction, Wormwood Scrubbs, and on entering the Stadium.

The countries represented in the Race will be—

United Kingdom · Canada
United States · Australia
Holland · Sweden · South Africa
Greece · Finland · Russia
Belgium · Italy · Germany
Austria · Bohemia
Denmark.

In order that the competitors may not be impeded by traffic, a force of two thousand police will guard the course.

The public in the Stadium will not be kept in ignorance of the progress of the Race until the leader bursts into the arena for the final lap. Elaborate telephoning arrangements have been made, and the names and progress of the leading men will be shown every few minutes. The sports in the arena will be stopped and the track cleared when the approach of the runners is announced.

THE great event in the Olympic Games is the Marathon Race on Friday, and which, without doubt, will arouse greater International interest than any other of the great struggles at the Stadium. ... race through Windsor and Eton on their way to the Stadium. The King has given permission for the general public to assemble within the Castle Gates at the start of the race, and for the school children to congregate within the Castle ...

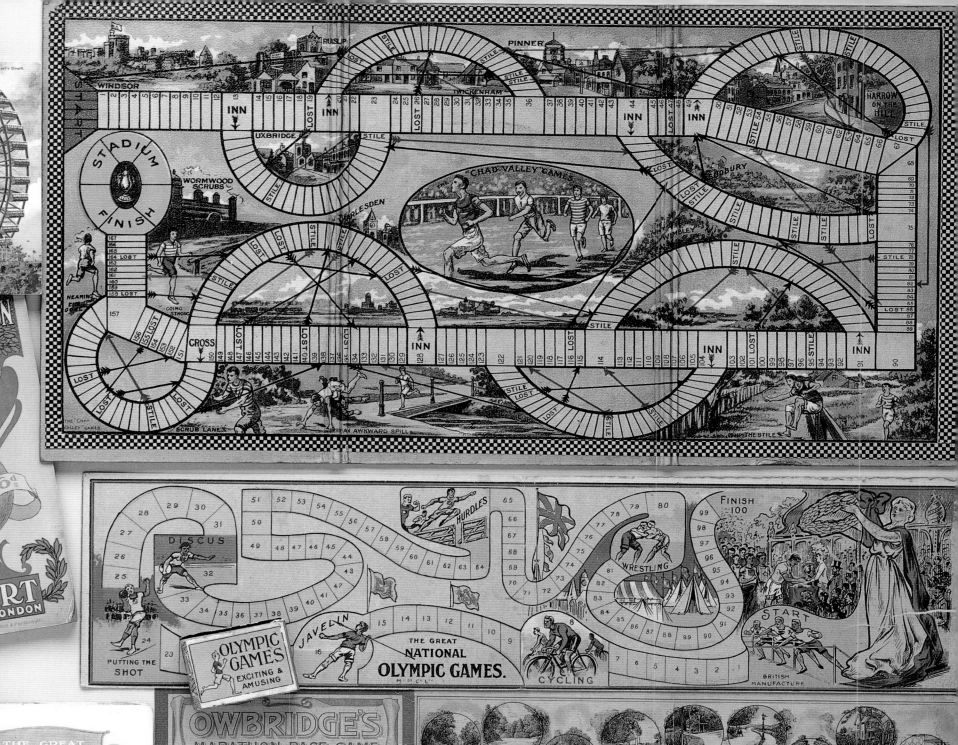

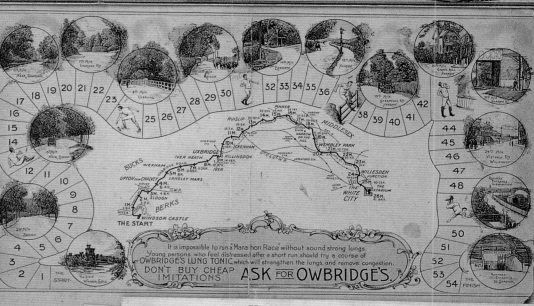

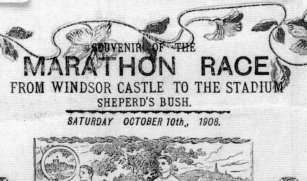

MARATHON RACE
FROM WINDSOR CASTLE TO THE STADIUM
SHEPERD'S BUSH.

SATURDAY OCTOBER 10th, 1908.

Guaranteed to contain 4 ounces of Tobacco when packed at the Factory SOLD SUBJECT TO LOSS BY EVAPORATION

Manufactured by GODFREY PHILLIPS LIMITED, LONDON, ENG.

BEST QUALITY

BEST QUALITY

4 OZ. TIN.

London was a focal point for international events; exhibitions were held at Earls Court, Olympia and Crystal Palace at Sydenham, home for the Colonial & Indian Exhibition of 1905. In 1908 the Great Stadium was built at Shepherds Bush to accommodate 60,000 spectators for the Olympic Games. Twenty-two nations took part; Britain won 56 gold medals over the 22 of USA. It was the Marathon which caught the public imagination. Run from Windsor Castle the leading runner, Dorando Petri, was disqualified for receiving help. Subsequently, he received a special cup from Qu. Alexandra (see above). **57**

FRANCO-BRITISH EXHIBITION. MARCH.

By OSCAR VERNE.

LONDON
W. PAXTON. 95. NEW OXFORD STREET. W.C
BLOCK ARCADE

1361

Franco-British Exhibition
London (Shepherd's Bush)
1908
Official Guide

SPECIAL EXHIBITION NUMBER.
DAILY MAIL.
Daily Circulation Five Times as Large as That of Any Penny London Morning Journal

FARROW'S BANK LTD.
(THE PEOPLE'S BANK)
THE HOME OF PEOPLE'S BANKING IN ENGLAND.

PROSET
(GOOD HEALTH)
NATURE'S NATURAL DRINK.
The New NON-ALCOHOLIC FRUIT BEVERAGE
EXTRA DRY
Bottled only by SCHWEPPES LTD

FRANCO-BRITISH EXHIBITION 1908
SHEPHERD'S BUSH LONDON

OFFICIAL DAILY PROGRAMME
PRICE 3D

Franco-British Exhibition
Official Souvenir

THEY TOLD ME I SHOULD ENJOY MYSELF AT THE EXHIBITION.
Donald McGill

The Flip-Flap.
Franco-British Exhibition, London, 1908

THE COURT OF HONOUR BY DAY
The buildings with their innumerable pinnacles and minarets, the dainty little pavilions that jut out from the bridge and from the shore, are of pure Indian architecture, resembling the Taj Mahal at Agra.

BRITISH TEXTILES BUILDING
The main entrance to this building is in the Court of Honour. Here the leading textile manufacturers of Great Britain exhibit their silks, linens, cotton and woollen goods in an attractive manner.

I SAW THIS LAST NIGHT AT THE EXHIBITION — WAS IT YOU?
Donald McGill

Bird's-eye-View, Franco-British Exhibition, London 1908.

THE PALACE OF MUSIC
This particularly handsome edifice has been specially erected for holding concerts and functions which cannot be given in the Congress Hall. A flower show was recently held here. The hall contains a spacious platform at one end, and can comfortably seat an audience of 2,000.

The Prince of Wales opened the Franco-British Exhibition on 14th May 1908, and the wealth of two nations went on display to cement the Entente Cordiale signed in 1904. The 200 acre site at London's Shepherds Bush contained 25 palaces and halls, and was attended by 8.4 million visitors. It became known as the White City. The Daily Mail had installed a printing machine capable of producing 200,000 four-page newspapers per hour. One of the novel attractions was the 'Flip-Flap', two gigantic steel arms 150 feet long each supporting a viewing platform that carried 50 people. Each arm would rise till they met virtically alongside each other. Donald McGill caught the question of the year, 'Would you like to flip-flap with me?'

58

- **1901**
  Edward VII became King (22nd January) on death of Q.Victoria
  Nobel Prizes first awarded
  Imperial Tobacco Company formed
  Marconi sent wireless signals across Atlantic
  Mixed bathing allowed, at Bexhill
  First driving school opened
  Kodak's Brownie camera available in Britain

- **1902**
  Coronation of King Edward VII
  Boer War finally over
  Vacuum cleaner launched
  Peter Rabbit published by Warne
  New brands included Marmite, Frys
  milk chocolate and Force wheat flakes.

- **1903**
  Mrs Pankhurst formed Women's Social and Political Union
  Motor Car Act passed
  Daily Mirror launched
  Teddy bears on sale
  New brands included Perrier table water and Typhoo Tipps Tea

- **1904**
  Entente Cordiale signed
  First electric underground line
  Underground ticket machine introduced
  Postage stamp books issued
  613 million postcards delivered
  James Barrie's Peter Pan play opened
  Vim scouring powder launched

- **1905**
  Automobile Association (AA) founded
  Gillette safety razor and
  Heinz baked beans came from USA
  Aspirin arrived (made by Bayer)
  Brasso metal polish on market

- **1906**
  HMS Dreadnought launched
  Austin motor cars on sale
  First Grand Prix, held at Le Mans
  Bournville Cocoa available

- **1907**
  Brooklands motor-racing track opened
  Boy Scout movement founded
  Meccano, previously called
  Mechanics Made Easy since 1901

- **1908**
  Franco-British Exhibition
  Olympic Games at White City
  First aircraft in Britain
  First Daily Mail Ideal Home Exhibition
  Underground map with different colours for each line
  Police dogs on the beat
  First international beauty contest held
  The Magnet and The Scout publications
  Shredded Wheat came from USA

- **1909**
  Bleriot's aeroplane crossed English Channel
  British aviation contests held
  Old Age Pensions paid: 5/- a week to those 70 years and over
  Daily Sketch launched
  Selfridges store opened in London
  First Woolworths opened, in Liverpool
  American Robert Peary reached North Pole
  New brands included Ovaltine and Persil

- **1910**
  Death of Edward VII (16th May)

Opposite: hospital appeal poster, c1905

In 1907 a permanent international health organisation was established; two years later in Britain a proposal was put forward for a unified state medical service for everyone.

Advertising postcards spread the manufacturer's message